BE A GOOD PARENT:
Guides and important tools for good parenting

Lamont C. Stone

Table of contents

Chapter 1

Chapter 2

Chapter 3

Chapter 4

Chapter 1

THE REALITY OF PARENTHOOD.

It's much harder than you thought to be a parent.In fact, the majority of parents believe that the most challenging stage of parenting is when their colicky baby is a newborn. Wait till your adolescent starts driving or dating, though.

You'll yearn for the times when whether or not your child napped was your top concern.Your children will reflect your flaws.You will observe these traits in your children, whether it be your high degree of irritability, your difficulty concentrating, your ongoing messiness, or your persistent procrastination.

You will also grimace at it. You will want to improve yourself after seeing these negative behaviors repeated a few times.You'll take cues from your own parents.The sluggish progression may cause you to miss it at first.

But then you'll be very shocked when you say something like, "Don't make me turn this automobile around," one day. You're now your mother (or father).You'll learn to communicate with infants.You will be your children's lone interpreter for a while, able to understand what they are saying.

As a result, you will essentially act as their interpreter and find yourself stating things like: "He is starving, she needs milk, or they are wary of bearded individuals. Sorry."Your entire life is changedYour Netflix account may eventually exclusively suggest children's programming.

This won't start happening to you until it does, all of a sudden. You finally have some time on a Friday night to relax and watch an adult program. However, the only things on your list of suggestions are Spongebob, Curious George, and the Disney princesses.Your main concern is no longer your dog.Before the arrival of the human baby, the poor tiny furry baby was the center of attention.

Now you'll be asking yourself, "When did I last fill the dog's bowl with fresh water?"You'll come to understand that folding baby garments is misery, sometimes much worse than folding a fitted sheet.You will need four times as long to fold and put away one basket of baby laundry. There are simply a ton of bits.

And that is frustrating!It will be difficult to converse with your pals who are childless.Nobody is to blame for it. It simply is. Your friends want to speak about their jobs, vacations, and the most recent book they are reading, while you want to talk about your kids, their accomplishments, and their activities—all the things you hardly have time for.

There will be many awkward pauses, and you'll feel bad for bringing up your children.Nothing makes you feel ashamed anymore.Nope.

Nothing. Not even nursing in public, singing to your crying baby on the train, or sending your child to school in your pajamas. These days, your concerns go beyond outward appearances.

You won't be able to relieve yourself in peace for a while.You may give up on ever using the bathroom without being interrupted, whether you have a baby in a bouncy chair next to you or a toddler knocking on the door.

As soon as you close the restroom door, even teenagers will need something or want to know where something is.You'll realize that the day is not long enough.Whether you have young children or teens, your to-do list is excruciatingly long due to your obligations, carpooling, and general running around

.Every day you manage to take a shower will feel like a success.Additionally, every journey outside the house—even if it's only to Target—will make you feel like you're getting ready for an international trip.

Do not feel guilty for acknowledging these successes.You Transform Into a Completely New Being.Your ninja abilities will improve.You will learn to slink in and out of situations like a ninja, whether it's sneaking out of the baby's room at night unobserved, sneaking into your preschooler's room to fetch your book, or getting up without awakening a sleeping child.You'll laugh more than you ever imagined you could.

Let's face it, infants are hilarious. Children are funny. They say and do the craziest things, making you laugh until your sides hurt at times.If it means purchasing a particular item for your child, you will put off spending money on yourself.And it will make you happier than you could have ever imagined. Moms have a reputation for dressing dated because of this.

The kids are receiving all of their financial resources.You'll learn to enjoy children's television and film.You will genuinely look forward to watching these shows, whether it is the Disney channel or the most recent Toy Story film.

Not so much because they provide excellent entertainment, but more because they are a wonderful way to relax and cuddle with the kids.Every stage of your life will see a change in your friendship circles.No matter how determined you are to keep your current friendships alive, some of them will end. It is simply a fact.

You might, for instance, give up going out or taking weekend trips in favor of spending more time with the mothers at your neighborhood playgroup. You might become friends with some PTA parents or the parents of your child's travel sports team when your children get older.

Nobody is to blame for it. Simply put, that's how life is.You might find the children of others annoying.You already have to deal with your own children's snot, tantrums, puke, and complaining.

Your ability to tolerate other children may be nonexistent.Your wardrobe is mostly made up of sweaters, sweatpants, and leggings.You never imagined yourself in this situation, yet it has happened. You're dressed as a conventional parent or parent figure. After all, you are frequently too exhausted to care.

So you choose cotton, comfort, and simplicity.More than you ever imagined humanly possible, you worry.Who knows what will fill your mind?

There is never a time when you are not worried about something, from the early stages of motherhood when you are worried about your baby's pooping, urinating, and nursing habits to the later stages when you worry about texting and driving, dating, and grades.After-natal CareYour personal possessions will be destroyed.

Your car's backseat will be downright revolting.Despite how frequently you clean your car, there is always juice on the floor, smashed Cheerios and Goldfish, and a mountain of toys, extra diapers, and other clutter. Even when your children are older, you will still be annoyed by their musty sports equipment and McDonald's wrappers from all the carpooling. Never again will your car be the same.

Your kids will get their dirty hands on your iPhone despite the vows you make to yourself.Additionally, their baby slobber may damage your battery. They'll break into your Facebook account when they're older and post arbitrary selfies of themselves. No matter how hard you try, everything you own, even your priceless iPhone, becomes their property.You'll destroy your beloved sweater, pair of pants, or jacket.It could be baby poop, sticky fingers, or even a teen's first time attempting to do the laundry. However, you won't find it as annoying as you could.

Oh, you could be a little irritated at first, but the subsequent wide grin or firm squeeze will make all of your annoyance disappear.You'll have a different relationship with food.Most of your meals will be consumed either quickly or while you are still standing at the counter.You simply don't have the time to eat a leisurely lunch because someone will need their diaper changed right as you do. You will find yourself eating on the go even when the kids are older and you are driving them from A to B.You'll discover how to sneak candy and other delicacies into the house while passing them off as illicit substances.

However, your children will have canine-like noses and be experts at sniffing out chocolate. You'll thus resign yourself to shoving whole chocolate bars into your mouth while huddling in the laundry room, or you'll resign yourself to stowing them in the freezer inside a used broccoli bag.

You'll consume more "child food" than you ever imagined.Before having children, you might not have touched a package of manufactured macaroni and cheese or a chicken nugget. That doesn't mean you won't do it now.

Sometimes you simply don't have enough time to prepare the salad you ought to eat.

As a result, you consume what the kids are eating and act as though it tastes nice.You'll Be AstoundedPoop is everywhere.Nobody warns you about the volume of feces you will encounter. In fact, young children in good health may poop three times every day. It stinks that kids are no longer being breastfed or given formula and are instead consuming solid foods. Truly really stinks, like.

 Additionally, you have to deal with it every day. Even when they are adults, the restroom odor could make you dizzy.It can be lonely to be a parent.Nobody warns you about how incredibly lonely it may be. In actuality, it makes little difference whether you are a working or stay-at-home mother. The majority of your leisure time is spent caring for your children. For this reason, it is crucial to schedule adult time whenever you can.

Even if it's simply a friend and a cup of coffee while the infant sleeps upstairs.It will never be the same in your marriage.A marriage may suffer greatly from life after children.

Finding time alone together suddenly becomes absurdly challenging, especially if money for babysitting is limited. Initially, you could try to schedule date evenings when the infant snoozes, but you frequently discover that you are too worn out to really have a thoughtful conversation.

Then, as the kids become older and remain up later, you start looking through the family schedule for brief moments to be private.Being a parent is so dull and routine.For many parents, this fact comes as a major culture shock.

It can get very boring to repeat the same activities day after day after the novelty of the infant wears off.

Anyone would go insane from the constant cycle of feeding, sleeping, and diaper changes.Your kids will face scrutiny for the rest of their life

Chapter 2

CAUSES OF TERRIBLE PARENTING

Bad parenting may be characterized as inadequate assistance from parents for their children in an emotional, psychological, intellectual or physical sense.

If your parents are addicted to legal drugs like alcohol or illicit drugs, they may no longer be able to take care of you in a proper way as drug abusers frequently think more about how they can secure their substance supply than about taking care of their children.

Therefore, if you grow up in a family where your parents take drugs, you may suffer from severe neglect.

Unwanted child

Some parents are pretty thrilled to receive children. However, some parents are not prepared for it and their children are more a type of accident.

These so-called unwanted children will frequently not be treated that well as parents haven't intended to obtain them and may not be prepared to take care of these youngsters.

Moreover, these parents may also not be able to raise their children in a good way as they just haven't prepared themselves and do not know what's vital.

Egoism

Some parents are also highly egotistic and care far more about themselves and their advancement in life than about the mental and physical well-being of their children.

If you grow up in such a home, chances are that you may suffer from severe neglect and other mental difficulties as you may not feel worthwhile at all.

This issue gets considerably worse if egoism goes into high degrees of narcissistic conduct of parents.

Mental difficulties

Parents with mental health disorders may also not be able to take care of their children in an appropriate way.

For instance, if your parents suffer from mental difficulties like hallucinations or schizophrenia, chances are that they would rarely be able to handle their own life and you as a kid will have to take care of yourself from a pretty early age on.

Mental disorders of parents may also result in physical health concerns for children if these mental problems induce parents to mistreat their children.

Physical health difficulties

Parents may also not be able to assist their children in a satisfactory way owing to physical impairments.

For instance, if your parents depend on a wheelchair to get about, they will not be able to go shopping or to cook for you as a youngster.

They may also not be able to bring you to school and their impairment may hinder them to do various other chores in their everyday lives.

Therefore, your parents may not be able to take care of you in a suitable way.

You as a youngster may even have to support them instead.

Poverty

Another factor for terrible parenting may be poverty.

If you grow up in a home where poverty is a huge problem, chances are that your parents may not be able to guarantee you with good education and other things that might boost your prospects for your future life.

Poverty may also lead to high levels of pessimism and frustration for your parents, which may raise the possibility of child abuse or other detrimental repercussions for their children.

Unemployment

Unemployment may be another issue when it comes to lousy parenting.

If your parents are jobless, your family may suffer from considerable levels of poverty, which may hinder you from acquiring good schooling, particularly if you reside in a poor developing nation.

Moreover, unemployment may also lead to mental health concerns for your parents, which may further raise the chance of bad child-rearing.

Additionally, additionally your chances of getting jobless once you grow up grow, as youngsters copy many qualities of their parents and may behave similarly once they develop into adults.

Overtaxing

Parents may also be somewhat overwhelmed by the sheer quantity of labor children normally require.

Therefore, some parents may not be able to cope with all these challenges and may also not be ready to put in all this effort.

This may lead to neglect and various other troubles for the respective youngsters.

Career aspirations

In many firms, even while companies profess to encourage the private lives of workers, it is still fairly challenging to mix a family with an ambitious job.

Therefore, in homes where both parents have a hard profession, children may suffer due to it as their parents would work very long hours and may not be able to take care of their children in an adequate way.

Divorce

A divorce is a very unpleasant occurrence that may convert into various complications, including conflicts over monetary possessions but also regarding who would be liable to take care of the children.

If this conflict goes out of hand, children may frequently have to grow up with just one parent and may suffer from this in an emotional sense.

Frustration

Depending on numerous factors, life might be rather challenging for certain individuals.

People may frequently feel to be treated unjustly by religion and may get extremely desperate and frustrated owing to blows of destiny or other significant unfavorable situations.

This desperation may develop into irritation, which may translate into child abuse as some parents are not able to cope with the circumstance in an emotionally healthy way.

Lack of education

The manner of parenting also substantially impacts the degree of schooling of children.

If parents are quite eager to provide their children with education materials and also help them with their homework, chances are that these children will be able to get better grades and to attend better schools and colleges compared to children from families where their parents do not care too much about the education of their children.

The requirement for a good parent plus kid affair

Positive ties between parents and children are vital for all aspects of children's development.

Positive connections with children are founded on being in the present, spending quality time and creating trust.

Your bond with your kid will vary and expand as your child grows and develops.

Being in the present is about tuning in and thinking about what's going on with your kid. It tells your kid that you care about the things that are important to them, which is the cornerstone for a successful connection.

Show acceptance, let your kid be, and try not to provide orders all the time. If your youngster wants to imagine the construction blocks are humans, that's OK. You don't have to get your youngster to use them in the 'right' manner.

Notice what your youngster is doing and remark on or encourage it without judgment. For example, 'Are the huge blue blocks the shopkeepers? And is the small red block going shopping?'

Listen to your youngster and attempt to tune in to your child's true sentiments. For example, if your kid is giving you a lengthy tale about lots of things that occurred throughout the day, they could truly be stating that they enjoy the new teacher or that they're in a good mood.

Stop and think about what your child's conduct is telling you. For example, if your adolescent kid is hanging about in the kitchen but not talking much, they could simply want to be near to you. You may provide a hug or let them assist with the cooking, without having to chat.

Part of being in the now with your kid is providing your youngster the opportunity to take the lead. For example:

Let your kid lead play by monitoring your child and reacting to what your child says or does. This is wonderful for younger children.

Support your child's ideas. For example, if your older kid wishes to host a family supper, why not say yes?

When your kid offers an opinion, you might utilize the dialogue as an opportunity to learn more about your child's views and emotions, even if they're different from yours.

Special moments with children.

Positive interactions between you and your kid are founded on meaningful time. Time together is how you learn to know about one other's experiences, ideas, emotions, and shifting interests. This demonstrates that you care and appreciate your kid, which is fantastic for your connection.

Quality time may happen anytime and everywhere, amid routine days and circumstances. It might be a shared chuckle while you're washing your toddler or a pleasant talk in the vehicle with your teenage kid. These times provide you the ability to send good messages through smiles, laughing, eye contact, embraces and soft touches.

You can make the most of time together by eliminating disturbances and distractions. This may be as simple as putting aside your phone. It lets your youngster realize that you're truly eager to spend undisturbed time with them.

There can be moments in your family life when it's not feasible to spend a lot of time with your kid every day. But organizing some regular one-on-one time with your youngster might help you make the time count.

Your kid learns and grows via spending time and interacting with you and other caretakers. For example, the time you spend chatting with your kid in the first three years of life helps your youngster acquire language.

Trust and respect: how to cultivate it in healthy relationships

Trust and respect are fundamental to a strong parent-child connection.

In the early years with your infant, creating trust is vital. Your infant will feel confident when they realize they can trust you and other important caretakers to satisfy their requirements. This feeling of protection and stability gives your youngster confidence to explore the world.

Trust and respect become more of a two-way street as your kid grows older.

You may foster trust and respect in your relationship. For example:

Be there when your kid needs support, care or aid. This may be scooping up your toddler when they fall, or picking up your adolescent kid when they phone you after a party. This helps your youngster grow to trust that you'll be there when they need you.

Chapter 3

THE NEED FOR A HEALTHY PARENT AND CHILD RELATIONSHIP

being in the moment with your child spending quality time with your child creating a caring environment of trust and respect.

There's no formula for getting your parent-child relationship right. But if your relationship with your child is built on warm, loving, and responsive interactions most of the time, your child will feel loved and secure.

Being in the moment: how it supports positive parent-child relationships
Being in the moment is about tuning in and thinking about what's going on

with your child. It shows your child that you care about the things that matter to them, which is the basis for a strong relationship.

Here are some ideas for being in the moment with your child:

Show acceptance, let your child be, and try not to give directions all the time. If your child wants to pretend the building blocks are people, that's OK. You don't have to get your child to use them the 'right' way.
Notice what your child is doing and comment on or encourage it without judgment. For example, 'Are the big blue blocks the shopkeepers? And is the little red block going shopping?'
Listen to your child and try to tune in to your child's real feelings. For

example, if your child is telling you a long story about lots of things that happened during the day, they might really be saying that they like the new teacher or that they're in a good mood. Stop and think about what your child's behavior is telling you. For example, if your teenage child is hanging around in the kitchen but not talking much, they might just want to be close to you. You could offer a hug or let them help with the cooking, without needing to talk.

Part of being in the moment with your child is giving your child opportunities to take the lead. For example:

Let your child lead play by watching your child and responding to what your child says or does. This is great for younger children.

Support your child's ideas. For example, if your older child decides to plan a family meal, why not say yes? When your child expresses an opinion, you could use the conversation as a way to learn more about your child's thoughts and feelings, even if they're different from yours.

Special moments with children
View video transcript (PDF: 36.7 KB)
This short video features parents talking about special moments with their children. They talk about how these moments build relationships and help them bond with their children. They also describe how love and affection help their children feel safe and secure.

Repeating or rephrasing your child's words, smiling, and making eye contact tell your child you're paying attention when you're talking or spending time together. These expressions of warmth and interest help your child feel secure and build confidence.

'Quality time': why it's important in positive relationships
Positive relationships between you and your child are built on quality time. Time together is how you get to know about each other's experiences, thoughts, feelings, and changing interests. This shows that you value and appreciate your child, which is great for your relationship.

Quality time can happen anytime and anywhere, in the middle of ordinary days and situations. It can be a shared laugh when you're bathing your toddler or a good conversation in the car with your teenage child. These moments give you the chance to communicate positive messages with smiles, laughter, eye contact, hugs, and gentle touches.

You can make the most of time together by minimizing disruptions and distractions. This can be as easy as putting away your phone. It helps your child know that you're really keen to spend uninterrupted time with them.

There might be times in your family life when it's not possible to have a lot of time with your child every day. But planning some regular one-on-one time with your child can help you make the time count.

Your child learns and develops through spending time and interacting with you and other carers. For example, the time you spend talking with your child in the first three years of life helps your child learn the language.

Trust and respect: how to nurture it in positive relationships
Trust and respect are essential to a positive parent-child relationship.

In the early years with your baby, developing trust is important. Your baby will feel secure when they learn they can trust you and other main carers to meet their needs. This sense of safety and security gives your child the confidence to explore the world.

Trust and respect become more of a two-way street as your child gets older.

You can nurture trust and respect in your relationship. For example:

Be available when your child needs support, care or help. This might be picking up your toddler when they fall, or picking up your teenage child when they call you after a party. This helps your child learn to trust that you'll be there when they need you.
Stick to your promises, so your child learns to trust what you say. For example, if you promise that you'll go

to a school activity, do everything you can to get there.

Get to know your child and value them for who they are. If your child loves football, cheer your child on or ask about the best players. Showing respect for your child's feelings and opinions encourages your child to keep sharing them with you.

When your child expresses a different opinion from yours, listen without judging or getting upset. This sends the message that you'll listen and help your child with difficult issues or situations in the future.

Allow the relationship to evolve as your child develops, and your child's needs and interests change. For example, your pre-teen child might no longer want you around at the park with their friends, even though your child used to love playing there with you.

Set up some firm but fair family rules. Rules are clear statements about how your family wants to look after and treat its members. They can help your child trust that you'll be consistent in the way you treat them.

Chapter 4

SORTING OUT IMPEDIMENTS TO TERRIBLE PARENTING AND BEING A GOOD PARENT.

Give your youngster lots of love. Attempt to build a deep physical and emotional relationship with your kid during their whole upbringing. A warm touch or a nice remark might let your youngster know how much you actually care about them. Here are some methods to display love and affection:

Cuddle your kid, a kiss on the cheek, a huge embrace, or even just a warm touch on the shoulder to offer encouragement and gratitude.

Tell them you love them every day, even if you're furious with them.

Love your children unconditionally. Don't push them to be who you believe they should be to win your affection. Let them know that you will always adore them no matter what.

For instance, you could hope that your kid would be sporty. If they're not particularly interested in sports, however, it's vital to let them know that that's acceptable, and work with them to find an activity that better matches their interests.

Similarly, don't make your kid feel guilty if it takes them a long to warm up to others, even if you're quite outgoing yourself.

Emphasize the significance of experiences above things. Toys may occupy your kid for a time, but they will never allow them to feel loved and cared for like an attentive parent can. Instead, spend time taking your kid to do exciting things—even something as simple as enjoying an ice cream cone in the park may build a lovely memory that will endure far longer than any item.

Even simply laying on the floor reading together may be a terrific bonding moment for you and your children.

Praise your children for their successes. Help your kids feel proud of their successes and good about themselves. When they accomplish something excellent, let them know that you've noticed and that you're really pleased with them. If you don't give them the confidence they need to go out in the world on their own, then they won't feel empowered to be independent or adventurous.

Be precise in your compliments to let them know exactly what is being appreciated. For example, instead of responding, "Good job!" you may say, "You did fantastic taking turns with your sister while playing," or "Thank you for cleaning up the toys after playing with them!"

Make it a point to praise your children's achievements and good conduct more than their inherent gifts. That will help children learn to respect taking on a big task.

Try to get in the habit a habit of praising your children more frequently than you offer them negative comments. Though it's vital to inform your children when they're doing something wrong, it's equally crucial to helping them establish a good sense of self. In addition, if you concentrate too much on poor conduct, your children may act out more to obtain your attention]

Avoid comparing your children to others, particularly siblings. Each kid is special and unique, so cherish their peculiarities. If you frequently compare your child to other kids, it could make them feel that they can never be good enough in your eyes. It could even hold them back from achieving success later on. [6] Instead of comparing them to other kids, assist your children to learn how to fulfill objectives on their own terms, and encourage them to pursue the road that works for them.

Comparing one kid to their siblings might encourage your children to create a rivalry. Try to create a loving connection between your children, not a competitive one.

Don't exhibit preference amongst your children, either—if they're bickering, be fair and impartial.

Give your youngsters your entire attention while they're chatting. It's crucial to have open communication with your kids, so make sure you take the time to stop and listen when they come to you with questions or concerns. In addition, demonstrate an interest in your children and immerse yourself in their lives. This will assist establish an environment in which your children may come to you with an issue, whether great or minor.

Practice active listening with your children so they know you're paying attention to them. Look at them as they speak to you, and indicate to them you're following along by nodding and making positive remarks, such as "Uh huh," "I understand," or "Keep going." When it is your moment to speak, summarize what you heard them say before you react. For instance, you may remark, "It seems like you're suggesting that this week's task list is unjust."

Try putting up a designated time to chat with each kid every day. This might be before sleep, during breakfast, or on a stroll after school. Treat this time as sacrosanct and avoid checking your phone or being distracted.

Make one-on-one time for each youngster. It's incredibly vital for kids to feel like they're important to their parents, so consciously block out time to spend with each of your children. During that time, arrange something pleasant to do together, like going for a stroll, having a snack, or putting together a puzzle. While you're doing that, give your kid your whole attention—talk to them and listen to what they have to say. Even simply casually spending time together might be incredibly significant to them

Try to share your time even if you have more than one kid. However, bear in mind that you don't have to do the same thing with each one—maybe one of your children loves roller skating, for instance, while the other might be happy with a trip to the library.

Be involved with their studies as well. For example, when you can, try to attend school activities, complete homework with your children, and check their grades to get a feel of how they are doing in school. You may also join a Parent Teacher Association (PTA) if you'd want to be more active in their education.

Be cautious not to suffocate or smother your children, however—give them time to themselves, too. You want them to feel that your time together is exceptional, not like they're compelled to spend time with you.

Respect your child's privacy to create trust. Allow your children to believe that once they enter their room, no one will peek through their drawers, or read their diaries. This will educate kids to honor their own space and to respect the privacy of others. It will also provide children a feeling of stability, and it will help create trust between the two of you.

Allow your kid to preserve their personal space and recognize that it's acceptable for them to occasionally hold secrets from you, particularly as they become older. You can balance this by having an open door policy so that people may approach you if they need assistance with a problem.

Be present for the milestones. You may have a tight work schedule, but you should do all you can to be present for the critical milestones in your children's lives, from their ballet performances and birthdays through their high school graduation. Remember that children grow quickly and that they'll be on their own before you realize it. Your employer may or may not remember that you missed that meeting, but your kid will most surely remember that you didn't attend the play they were in.

If something occurs and you have to miss an important milestone, let your kid know that you're extremely sorry you missed it, and make it up to them with a special celebration. For instance, if you can't accompany your kid to class on the first day of school, you may celebrate by buying up their favorite food and a special dessert that night.

Being a Good Disciplinarian

Enforce fair rules and penalties. Create a set of family rules that will help your children experience a happy, productive life. Make sure these guidelines are acceptable for your child's age. Remember, your rules and guidelines should help your kid learn and thrive, but they shouldn't be so rigid that they feel like they can't do anything correctly.

For example, if you have a smaller kid, you may set guidelines like "Don't go outdoors without an adult," with the penalty of being grounded inside if they breach that rule. For older children, you could create rules about assisting around the home, and you might take away a privilege like a screen time if they don't perform their duties.

Listen to your child's criticism about the rules they have to obey, but remember—you are the parent. Children require limits. A youngster who has been permitted to do as they wish may suffer in adult life when they have to respect society's laws.

Avoid unduly severe types of punishment, and never do anything that involves physically harming your child—in addition to being cruel, it may also make behavioral issues worse.] It's always best to support and advise your kid so they may learn from their error.

Be consistent with your rules. Even though it might be challenging occasionally, it's crucial to enforce the same rules all the time. Try not to let your youngster persuade you into creating exceptions. If you let your kid do something he or she is not permitted to do only because he or she is throwing a tantrum, then this indicates that your rules are breakable.

If your kid believes that your rules are breakable, they won't have a reason to keep to them.

Control your anger as much as you can. It's crucial to try to be as calm and rational as possible while you're dealing with your children, especially if they're misbehaving. Obviously, this may be quite a problem, particularly when your children are acting out or simply driving you up the wall, but if you feel yourself getting ready to raise your voice, take a break and excuse yourself, or at least let your kids know that you are about to become irritated.

We all lose our tempers and feel out of control, occasionally. If you do or say anything you regret, you should apologize to your children, letting them know that you've made a mistake. Teaching children to apologize and confess when they were wrong is a more vital lesson than appearing like you're alway